"HAPPY"

– Reloaded

Recode Your Mind
For Modern Happy Living

By:

MASTER JENNIFER W. YU

THE "MOMMA PANDA"

"HAPPY": n.

It's used as "The State of Happiness or Being Happy" in this book.

It's marked by a combination of internal feelings ranging from warmth, fuzziness, security, comfort, contentment, appreciation, gratitude, joy, lovingness, resolve, peace to bliss.

– Master Jennifer W. Yu/Momma Panda

To You

My Beloved Baby Pandas

You are my inspirations.

You are my blessings.

You are my HAPPY!

Written by:
Jennifer W. Yu

Drawings by:
Claudio Verzura

Edited & Proofed by:
Jason Wang & Brian Walsh

Cover Photo by:
Steve McPherson

Published by:
Best Seller Publishing & HAPPY TAI CHI™
www.bestsellerpublishing.org
www.happytaichi.org

ISBN 978-1-946978-59-2

1st edition in United States of America, January 2018

WARNING

This book may cause you to smile uncontrollably, evoke fond memories, warm thoughts, fuzzy emotions, and to move your body and mind in joyful ways. ☺

This book may also cause you to self-reflect and make changes in mind-style.

English is not Momma Panda's first language.

"Reader's discretion is advised." ☺

Any ideas or methods presented here are not medical prescriptions but personal opinions. It may be used as an adjunct, not replacement, to any current medical prescriptions, treatments, and therapies by healthcare and nutritional professionals. Please seek their advice before making changes.

CONTENTS

INTRODUCTION

WHEN A MAN LOST HIS HORSE

A farmer at a border Chinese village got up one morning and realized his only horse was missing. He fell into deep sadness. His horse was his most valued possession in the farm.

After many months of feeling depressed, he got up one morning and saw his precious horse returned and pregnant. Along with her, a strong mustang also joined the family farm. He was thrilled.

Farmer's only son started to train the mustang. One day he fell from the horse and broke both of his legs. The young man eventually became crippled leaving the farmer in deep sorrow again.

Sometime later, an invading war broke out. All the young men in the small village went to defend their land, except farmer's unwanted crippled son. At the end, no man made it back.

When a man lost his horse, how do you know it was not a good luck for him?

– Chinese parable

WHY "HAPPY"?

Happiness is the meaning and the purpose of life, the whole aim and end of human existence.

— Aristotle

I didn't know why I always had this strong attraction to the subject of happiness until I began to do my in-depth studies for my Healtheology dissertation of *How Tai Chi Effectively Improves Happiness*. I discovered that I had not been the only one.

I discovered that people around the world seemed to all agree with Aristotle and have put "To Be Happy" (HAPPY) at the top of their wish list. HAPPY is desired above wealth, position, social status, job success, sex, and fame.[1] In addition, statistics have shown that HAPPY appears to produce better health, longevity, relationships, prosperity, generosity, resilience and creativity.[1] This is probably why retaining and improving HAPPY are of the highest value to almost everyone.

Happiness is not only our right but clearly the principle force that drives our lives.

— Dalai Lama

It certainly made me happy to find out that we humans are like-minded when it comes to our desire to be happy. But soon my studies discovered that only less than 30% of people are reported deeply happy.[1] It hurts me to see the World Health Organization's prediction that by 2020 depression will be second only to heart disease in terms of the global burden of illness.[1]

You see, my busy Baby Panda, our fast-paced, over stimulating and more sedentary lifestyles today easily overwhelm us and create mental tensions. Human's pre-existing neurological condition of "over-sensitivity for the bad" from survival mechanisms of early evolution stage is making it worse. We tend to focus much more on "negativities", treat them as "threats", and react with tension or distress. The cumulative effect of daily trivial challenges and self-imposed worries continues to keep your neural system on red alert. This robs precious energy from your body and mind for recovery, detox and maintaining healthy homeostasis. As a result, chronic stress-induced health issues, both mental and physical, are related to almost all major ailments. Same goes with human social affairs, both domestically and globally. Human's quality of HAPPY is greatly compromised.

Thank goodness, studies have also shown that HAPPY can be measurably improved. It's believed that 40% of our HAPPY is under self-control. Better yet, recent findings have shown us that only 5% or less of cancers and vascular disease can be attributed to hereditary,[2] and that almost all major illnesses acquired are linked to chronic stress.[3-6] This suggests that almost all biological, mental and life activities, including our HAPPY, can be consciously improved. ☺

According to my recent "HAPPY" scores, I am one of those people who can be happy regardless what happens around me. Although that sounds great, I've come a long way. A challenging childhood in China, immigrating across the ocean to the U.S., and two abusive marriages caused me fear, worry, guilt, even total despair. Believe me, I know unhappiness first-hand. I also know I am not alone. People are suffering emotionally, mentally and physically all over the world. That's why I am compelled to study and write on this topic. I want to share my gift of transformation from darkness to happiness, which I achieved through the practice of Tai Chi.

You may think of Tai Chi as an exercise, a martial art or simply a mysterious Eastern concept. Soon you will learn the secret power it holds to bring wellness and HAPPY to your life just as a mindset.

WHY "HAPPY TAI CHI™"?

During one of my weekly calls with my son, Jason who is a Green Beret in the Army, I mentioned that I was pondering on the topics for my Ph.D. dissertation. I told him that I was thinking of writing about Tai Chi and I was also thinking of writing about my other favorite subject, improving happiness. He then asked why not combine the two and write about improving happiness with Tai Chi. It struck a chord in me. I immediately realized that among the extensive studies and reports on Tai Chi's mounting benefits for physical and mental health there had not been much writing or media focus on Tai Chi's benefits on HAPPY itself. The epidemic depression, addiction and unhappiness of modern people could really use this help. That's where it all began. It turned out that previous research had been more focused on various specific areas of physical and mental health. My study has discovered that Tai Chi's secret power to enhance HAPPY is the root cause and ultimate result of all its myriad benefits.

In his groundbreaking book, *The Biology of Belief*, biologist and epigenetics expert Bruce Lipton, Ph.D. has shown us that "perceptions determine biology." In other words, our own mindsets, habits and resilience in response to external stimuli ultimately create almost all of our own physical realities. Our brain has neuroplasticity. Our health and life can be bettered by simply switching to happier mindsets and more peaceful responses.

Inspired by both new findings and old wisdoms, drawn from 30 years of training, experiences, studies and insights on Tai Chi, wellness and happiness, Momma Panda has re-coded a new playbook for happy living in today's world. By alchemizing the proven effect of modern positive neuropsychology with the hidden power of ancient Tai Chi principles, HAPPY TAI CHI™ was born.

Reviewed by wellness professionals as the NGT (Next Great Thing) for modern happy living, HAPPY TAI CHI™ makes it much easier now for everyone to get to their "HAPPY" and to intersect distress at a neural level. You can simply plug it into your busy life as a mindset, a diet, a meditation, an exercise and/or a lifestyle as you see fit. Its insights and tips are simple and useful for any schedule, condition and situation. The same HAPPY strategy can be applied to health, relationship and business.

You will discover in this book that HAPPY TAI CHI™ is super charged with happy and harmonizing energy. It gives you "secret power" to enhance your current HAPPY and to combat the imbalance-induced distresses, clashes and unhappiness spreading in our modern societies. If you practice Momma Panda's HAPPY TAI CHI™ in any way, you will find yourself more balanced and healthier. You will definitely become happier. I promise you, my beloved new Baby Panda.

So, here's my gift to you, Momma Panda's HAPPY TAI CHI™ playbook for your ultimate "HAPPY".

HAPPY TAI CHI™ = Tai Chi + Smile

= Greater Homeostasis & Emotional Resilience

= Wellness (Serenity + Harmony + Prosperity)

= Your Ultimate "HAPPY"

WHY "MOMMA PANDA"?

Since I immigrated to the U.S. in 1989, I have personally taught tens of thousands of students, professionals, martial artists, world class athletes, homemakers, youth and retirees, ages 6 to 100. No matter the age, everyone is called "new baby" when first coming to my class.

Since I started HAPPY TAI CHI™, I began to feel more and more identified with panda's happy energy. Whenever I think of the panda bear, I become smiley instantly. So as time goes on, I have morphed into this "Momma Panda". If you read this book, you are now one of my beloved new "Baby Pandas".

Momma Panda

Baby Panda

DEDICATION

This book is dedicated to My Grandmother, Hu, Yuzi, a decedent of China's last emperor's royal clan and one of the earliest female educators in NE China, who had been ruthlessly tormented by Japanese invasion and communist prosecution through half of her life yet remained indomitable.

Dear Grandma, when you, as the dean of an elementary school at early 19th century, walked door to door in the snow with your previously bound and damaged feet to try convincing each father to let their daughters go to school, you did it with resolve.

When you were left with a family of 8 to support including one in your belly after grandpa's sudden death, you did it with resolve.

When you were let go for teaching Chinese by Japanese invaders at your university without your earned pension, and had to sell everything you owned to seek food and shelter in the countryside, you did it with resolve.

When you were classified as "Landlord" by the communist party due to the land you owned for food in the countryside, and facing the worst prosecution in China for you and all related to you, when you volunteered to go to the freezing Siberia to stay away from your loved ones hoping to save them, and when you lived in isolation and condemnation, swept the streets every morning, struggled to get water from a frozen well and carried it in blizzards a long way home, you did it all with resolve.

Amid all these unimaginable hardships, whenever there's a chance, you still taught little boys and girls including me how to read and write with love and HAPPY. You are a real life "HAPPY TAI CHI™" Master, grandma. I may not remember you in details, but whenever I look into the mirror, I see you. In the light of my eyes and the smile of my heart, your indomitable spirit shines right through me.

GRANDMA'S WEDDING PICTURE

GRANDMA'S FAMILY PICTURE WITH SIBLINGS

THE HAPPY TAI CHI MIND

MINDSET 1: ACCEPT QI & YOUR LIFE-SHIP

Qi (氣), aka Chi or Ch'i in English, is an old Chinese word pronounced *chee*.

What is Qi? Here's Momma Panda's short answer:

Qi = Energy

Vibrant Qi = Vibrant Life; Balanced Qi = Balanced Life.
Weak Qi = Weak Life; No Qi = No Life.

Qi is just Qi. Qi itself is benign. It flows in space, on earth, around us and inside our bodies. Every existence is a living and breathing generator-battery device powered by Qi. It is constantly absorbing, producing, processing, using, storing and releasing Qi all at the same time. It can and needs to be charged. It also can and needs to charge others. Without this ability and need, an electron, a cell, a person, a society, an entity, a nation, a planet, an event or any matter loses its ability and reason to exist as a part of this supply-demand energetic reality, which underlines and powers our grand visible landscape.

Qi is life's base currency. All lives need it, are naturally drawn to it, and are based on it. Life is a Qi play. To simply put it:

Qi = Energy = Life = Existence = Everything

Now, think of the Enterprise in the Star Trek movie for a moment. Imagine a huge "Enterprise" ship with all departments and crews on board, sailing in the water on Earth instead of in outer space. Qi is what keeps everyone's light on and all the systems running. Its quality and quantity directly determine the ship's rise and fall.

What if I tell you this amazing "Enterprise" is you? It has a bunch of specialized departments (bodily systems) and 50+ trillion dedicated crews (cells) working seamlessly around the clock.

If you have not realized this yet, please sit down now. Let Momma Panda take this moment to break this news to you. You are the chosen one, my beloved Baby Panda. Yes, YOU! You were born to be the Captain and Master of this mighty and ever-evolving "Enterprise". Perhaps your father, mother or other guardians had been running it for you in the past. But now, it's your time. You must accept your full duty to take charge of your almighty "Life-ship".

To sail your ship, my captain Baby Panda, you must first understand that everything runs on Qi. I mean everything. Qi is what keeps the universes moving, solar system spinning, earth rotating, cells forming, hearts pumping, ideas brewing, words effecting, laughter resonating, action taking, and above all, your ship sailing.

Accept your Qi & Life-Ship NOW, As-Is and Where-Is.

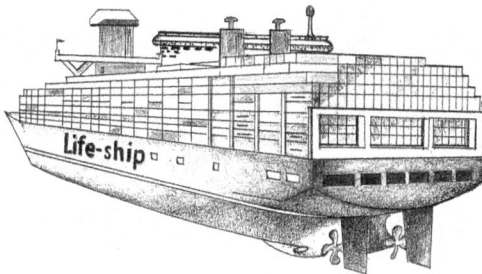

YOUR ALMIGHTY LIFE-SHIP

🐼 FUN GAME 1: QI TESTING

All energy manifests itself via different vibrations, waves, frequencies, light, heat, colors, electromagnetic fields, etc. Most energy can be measured and some can be physically sensed by humans. The flow of Qi inside and outside of the human body can be felt by most people in sensations of heat, warmth, coldness, tingles, magnetic-ness, bloating and/or numbness, especially on the most sensitive parts such as hands and fingers. Here are a couple of easy ways to test your Qi:

(Stand or Sit upright and be at ease.)

1. Passing the Qi:

- Hold your hands apart in front of waist, palms facing stomach (Pic 1 & 2).
- Slowly move hands closer until they pass by each other without touching (Pic 3 & 4).
- Slowly resume (Pic 2). Switch (Pic 5). Repeat a few times.

Pic 1

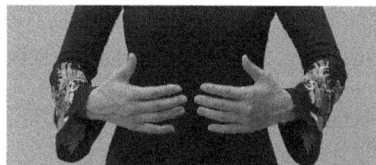

Pic 2

Pic 3

Pic 4

Pic 5

2. Twirling and Patting the Qi:

- Hold left arm up to the front, palm facing up. Put your right index finger above your left palm without touching (Pic 6). Twirl both ways (Pic 7 & 8).
- Use right hand to pat above and up-and-down left arm without touching (Pic 9).
- Switch. Twirl above the right palm and then pat the right arm (Pic 10).

PIC 7

PIC 8

PIC 9.1

PIC 9.2

PIC 6

PIC 9.3

PIC 10

How's your Qi at this moment? What did you feel?

Besides heat, I usually feel apparent sensations of tingling and static when the Qi field of my one hand enters and affects the Qi field of my other hand. The sensations typically get stronger after my Tai Chi practice.

It is harder to feel strong Qi sensations when it's very cold, windy, or when you feel weak. Don't be concerned if you don't feel anything initially. As your Qi flow and your sensitivity to it strengthen, your Qi feelings will become stronger and much easier to sense.

ACCEPTING vs. TOLERATING

Accepting is an act to acknowledge the existence of a life or situation on an equal ground with or without agreement or approval. Momma Panda thinks this act is of utmost importance to your HAPPY in two folds:

1. Accepting is a fundamental validation and implementation of our cherished constitutional belief of "all men are created equal",[7] which has united American people and produced our great progress and prosperity in the past 240 years.

2. Accepting empowers ownership and accountability by acknowledging that all current situations of us or our societies are the result of our past actions, and that all current actions of us or our societies as a whole are the causes for our future situations.

Every existence validates itself already by virtually existing as part of the divine, just like you and I. Only by first proactively accepting all divine existence as equal can we bring about clear understanding of the past, productive cooperation at the present and meaningful progress for the future.

Tolerating is an act to acknowledge the existence of a life or situation on a superior or rejecting ground with disapproval. Momma Panda thinks this act undermines your HAPPY in two folds:

1. Tolerating degrades the reason and purpose of a life or situation as inferior or less important. It's often due to its challenging nature caused by fear, lack of understanding and perception as burdens.

2. It demotes accountability as an individual, a group or a society by not taking full ownership of our past and current actions.

Every existence requires and longs for acceptance and validation, you and I included, my Baby Panda. Accepting is the first step towards HAPPY. Sail and let sail. Value all the quests on your journey, smooth or stormy. If you truly believe your way is healthier and happier, live it as a great example and share it. No coercion is needed. Other Life-ships will join you.

🐼 FUN GAME 2: ACCEPT YOUR LIFE-SHIP

No matter what condition it is currently in – super, good, so-so, rough or a total wreck, this ship is yours. She needs you to bring her to the best she can be. You need her for your long journey home.

Go over the current conditions of your Life-ship and accept one at a time:

Qi Connections:	Super	Good	So-So	Rough	Bad/None
With Divine	-----	-----	-----	-----	-----
With Self	-----	-----	-----	-----	-----
With Mate	-----	-----	-----	-----	-----
With Mom	-----	-----	-----	-----	-----
With Dad	-----	-----	-----	-----	-----
With Siblings	-----	-----	-----	-----	-----
With Kids	-----	-----	-----	-----	-----
With Co-Workers	-----	-----	-----	-----	-----
With Neighbors	-----	-----	-----	-----	-----
With Servicers	-----	-----	-----	-----	-----
With Peers	-----	-----	-----	-----	-----
With Strangers	-----	-----	-----	-----	-----
With Animals	-----	-----	-----	-----	-----
With Money	-----	-----	-----	-----	-----
-----------	-----	-----	-----	-----	-----
-----------	-----	-----	-----	-----	-----

Qi Departments:	Super	Good	So-So	Rough	Bad/None
Neurological	-----	-----	-----	-----	-----
Endocrine	-----	-----	-----	-----	-----
Cardiovascular	-----	-----	-----	-----	-----
Immunity	-----	-----	-----	-----	-----
Digestion	-----	-----	-----	-----	-----
Detoxification	-----	-----	-----	-----	-----
Skeletal/Joints	-----	-----	-----	-----	-----
Muscular	-----	-----	-----	-----	-----
-----------	-----	-----	-----	-----	-----

FIGURE 1: CATEGORIES OF QI SOURCES

Your Qi-powered Life-ship travels on Earth, under the stars, and among fellow Life-ships. You get your Qi from all 3 categories of sources:

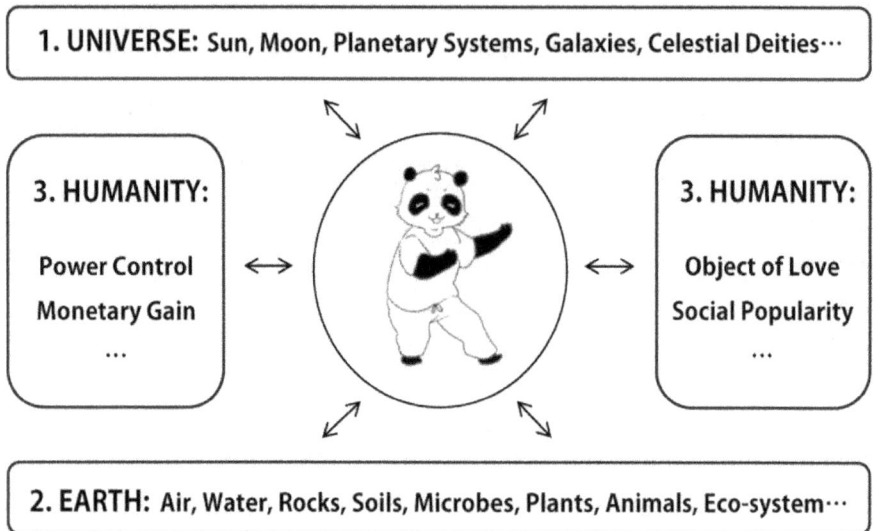

1. UNIVERSE: Sun, Moon, Planetary Systems, Galaxies, Celestial Deities···

3. HUMANITY:

Power Control

Monetary Gain

···

3. HUMANITY:

Object of Love

Social Popularity

···

2. EARTH: Air, Water, Rocks, Soils, Microbes, Plants, Animals, Eco-system···

Since the operation of your Life-ship solely depends on the continued supply of Qi, you must continuously generate Universal Qi from the Divine above, Humanity Qi from the people around, and Earthy Qi from the land under. Lack of any of the 3 will negatively affect the quality of your life. So, go ahead, my Baby Panda. Embrace and enjoy your higher powers, mother earth and fellow beings. They all are your Qi suppliers and barterers. So are you to them.

Every manifestation is a Qi holder with certain Qi exchange value. The more Qi it contains, the more precious it is. Compare a chair hand carved with a mass produced chair from a factory. Everyone will be attracted to the one holding more Qi. The top 4 sources for Humanity Qi are Power, Money, Fame and Object of Love. That's why people are naturally drawn to them.

To best supply and barter Qi with other Life-ships, give priority to the circles of Qi sources that are most relevant to your journey. First understand what others want. Ask yourself where your Qi is most needed and valued. Then provide and enhance your Qi exchange value, whether that is your precious ideas, info, resources, words, skills, feelings, actions or time.

🐼 FUN GAME 3: YOUR QI INCOMES AND EXPENSES

List Top 5 Things/Thoughts/Feelings/Activities **energizing** you: scale of 1-5

1. _____   _____

2. _____   _____

3. _____   _____

4. _____   _____

5. _____   _____

List Top 5 Things/Thoughts/Feelings/Activities **consuming** your Qi: 1-5

1. _____   _____

2. _____   _____

3. _____   _____

4. _____   _____

5. _____   _____

If "1" being very exhausted, "5" being very energized, on a scale of 1-5:

What's your average weekday Qi Level? _____ weekend? _____

If your Qi level is below 2, add more Things/Thoughts/Feelings/Activities energizing you to your routines; if your Qi level is at 5 all the time and you find hard to relax, add more Things/Thoughts/Feelings/Activities consuming your Qi to your life.

All your thoughts, words, feelings and actions are produced by Qi and also contain Qi. So, please remember, my beloved Baby Panda:

Words are Qi. They can heal and kill. Choose the words you speak.

MINDSET 2: HARNESS YOUR DUAL ENGINES

After you eagerly or reluctantly took ownership of your "Enterprise" ship and figured out the status of your ship's Qi level, it's time to acquaint and check on the "Dual Engines" running your Life-ship. One is called Yin (阴), pronounced *Yin*. One is called Yang (阳), pronounced *Young*.

Your Engine Yang is your Life-ship's driver for power-on, running-growing mode, heating, drying and all linear, logical and scientific applications. Your Engine Yin powers systems for switch-off, resting-repairing mode, cooling, humidifying, and all creative, intuitive and artistic programs. Don't be baffled by their foreign names. Both Yin and Yang are old Chinese words and abstract concepts used for thousands of years representing the dual tendencies and aspects of all existence. Just remember. Yang engine and its fuels bring the Qi up, outward, hot, tense, intellectual, industrious and logical; Yin engine and its fuels bring the Qi down, inward, cool, relaxing, sensible, artistic and intuitive. You will grasp quickly. ☺

Imagine you wake up in the morning from a restful nightly sleep, thanks to a well-working Yin engine. Your dutiful Yang engine kicks up and running. It deals with your peers or competitors, focuses on your demanding tasks at work or school, and finishes your sports training or gym routines. Your Yin engine, in the meantime, keeps you cool under pressure, attends to others' feelings at work or school, gives you creative ideas, cooperates with teammates during your basketball game, and makes sure not to overdo at the gym. After you get home, Yin engine turns up. You slow down, get relaxed, chat and show affection with family, and then go to sleep. During this time, your Yang engine conducts intelligent conversation over dinner, checks kids' homework, pays bills, and keeps your heart pumping, body warm and ready for any emergency actions during sleep. These two are life-long partners running your Life-ship day and night.

As you can tell, my captain Baby Panda, your Yin and Yang engines are EQUALLY important. They are complimentary and imperative to each other. Depending on the changing conditions inside and outside of your ship, you often run one more than the other at times. But to keep your Life-ship afloat and in good shape to reach your final destination, both engines are always needed.

Your Life-ship is not the only one running on this dual engines system. All Life-ship are. So are our societies, world and universe. Everything relating to us human is subject to this duality.

THE STORY OF "WHEN A MAN LOST HIS HORSE"

You have read this story at the beginning of the book. Most Chinese people know this parable. Your culture most likely has your version of it. It's a classic case demonstrating how things in our lives are driven by the dual engines of Yin and Yang. They appear in polarizing characters and flux constantly. When apart, the duo complement, define and need each other. Together, they cover the whole spectrum. Yin and Yang are relative in degrees and are always measured differently by different minds. Also, one tendency always bears the possibility for the other and interchanges when reaching extreme. Hence, your left and right sides make up your whole body; your trash is likely someone's treasure; if you over train, you will end up with no training due to injury or sickness, which is the exactly opposite.

So, my beloved Baby Panda, when things seem so easy, prepare for challenges. When things are going against you, it's just brewing for your betterment and stride. Always remember this story:

When a man lost his horse, it just may be a good luck for him.

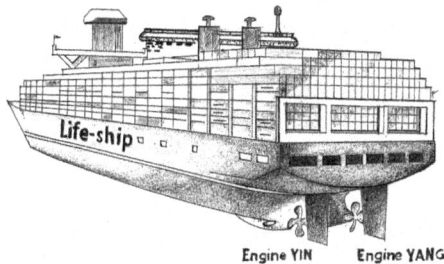

Engine YIN   Engine YANG

LIFE-SHIP WITH YIN AND YANG DUAL ENGINES

🐼 FUN GAME 4: COUNT YOUR RED AND BLACK BEANS

We are all born with a dual-engine system. Naturally, a male Life-ship is more Yang-oriented and a female Life-ship is more Yin-oriented. However, during the construction process of each ship, the wishes and body-mind food/fuels from the mom, dad and the surroundings can change the original settings. Let's take a Yin Yang inventory of our given body and the mind we have now.

Red Bean = YANG; Black Bean = YIN; If you feel extremely one way, give 2 beans; If only mildly, give 1 bean. If neutral, give 0 beans.

Body:	Red Bean	Black Bean
1. Bone Structure: (Strong/Broad/Thick – Red Bean; Delicate – Black Bean)	-----------	-----------
2. Skin: (Tough – Red Bean; Smooth/soft – Black Bean)	-----------	-----------
3. Face: (Masculine – Red Bean; Delicate/Feminine – Black Bean)	-----------	-----------
4. Hair: (Strong/Cut Short – Red Bean; Left Long/Soft – Black Bean)	-----------	-----------
5. Hands & Feet: (Strong/Big/Rough – Red Bean; Soft/Small/Pretty – Black)	-----------	-----------
6. Ring-Index Finger Ratio: (Ring>Index – Red Bean; Ring<Index – Black Bean)	-----------	-----------
7. Butt/Hips: (Sculpted/Small – Red Bean; Round/Bigger – Black Bean)	-----------	-----------
8. Body Hair/Muscles: (More – Red Bean; Less – Black Bean)	-----------	-----------
9. Breasts: (Smaller – Red Bean; Bigger – Black Bean)	-----------	-----------
10. Body's Gender: (Male – Red Bean; Female – Black Bean)	-----------	-----------

Total Beans =_____ = Total Red _____ + Total Blk _____

How Yang of a body were you born with?
Your Yang% = Total Red Beans /Total Beans x 100% = _____%
How Yin of a body were you born with?
Your Yin% = Total Black Beans /Total Beans x 100% = _____%

Mind:	Red Bean	Black Bean
1. Emotion: (More Rational – Red; More Emotional/Sensitive – Black)	_____	_____
2. Creativity: (More Scientific – Red; More Creative/Artistic – Black)	_____	_____
3. Speed: (Think/Decide/Move Fast – Red; Think/Move Slow – Black)	_____	_____
4. Activity: (More Active – Red; More Sedentary – Black)	_____	_____
5. Will-Power: (More Determined – Red; More Flexible – Black)	_____	_____
6. Focus: (Focus Well – Red; Distracted – Black)	_____	_____
7. Competition: (Competitive – Red; Avoid Competition – Black)	_____	_____
8. Bravery: (Protective – Red; Timid/Shy – Black)	_____	_____
9. Overall Mood: (Optimistic/Positive – Red; Cautious/Pessimistic – Black)	_____	_____
10. Mental Gender ID: (Identify as Male – Red; Identify as Female – Black)	_____	_____

Total Beans =_____ = Total Red _____ + Total Blk _____

How Yang is your mind right now?
Your Yang% = Total Red Beans /Total Beans x 100% = _____%

How Yin is your mind right now?
Your Yin% = Total Black Beans /Total Beans x 100% = _____%

FIGURE 2: LIFE'S DUALITY EFFECTS OF THE DUAL ENGINES

YANG Fuels/Results	YIN Fuels/Results
Big Bang	Black Hole
Particle	Wave
Sun	Moon
Summer	Winter
Day	Night
Heat	Cold
Acidity	Alkalinity
+Ion	-Ion
Science	Art
Hardness	Softness
Lead	Support
Growth	Reserve
Inhalation	Exhalation
Expansion	Contraction
Action	Rest
Rationality	Emotion
Ambition	Laidback
Strength	Flexibility
Confidence	Modesty
Logic	Intuition
Justice	Mercy
Right	Left
Up	Down
Open	Close
Fast	Slow
Fire	Water
Red	Green
Most Meat/Shell Fish	Most Veggies/Fruits
Table Sugar/Syrup	Salt
Spicy/Sour taste	Bitter/Salty taste
Coffee	Tea
...	...

YIN vs. YANG

Which is better? Which is more important? Which is more valuable?

Look at the list on the prior page. You may favor some over the others. But I am sure you can appreciate the value and the importance of both attributes.

Can you imagine if the Sun won't go down or if it won't come up again?

Can you imagine everyone wants to lead but no one wants to support and cooperate?

Can you imagine to keep on moving without stopping?

Can you imagine there is only science but no art whatsoever?

So, you may be drawn to favor more Yang or Yin engine based on your changing needs and situations. But just like your inhalation and exhalation, both are equally imperative and precious to you and all lives. The over use and extreme of one end will lead to the other.

Heaven needs Yin and Yang;
Earth needs softness and hardness;
Humanity needs mercy and justice;
These Three Marvels are interrelated and
based on the balance of the two opposites.

– I Ching (aka Yi Jing 易经, pronounced *Yee Ging*, Book of Change, 24th Century B.C.)

MINDSET 3: PLAY WITHIN 70/30 BOUNDARY

The secret playbook for your dual engines is called Tai Ji. What does it mean?

Tai Ji (太极), aka Tai Chi or T'ai Ch'i in English, is pronounced *Tie Gee* and means Grand Polarity. It's another old Chinese word used for thousands of years, hinting on the secret of life's hidden operating system. Here's Momma Panda's short definition:

Tai Ji/Tai Chi = Balancing Life's Yin and Yang Engines

Most male Life-ships are created more Yang-oriented while most female Life-ships are created more Yin. The goal is to balance the use of your engine Yin and engine Yang towards 50/50 or 60/40. In reality, the balance is never static, sometimes needing your Yin engine more and sometimes using Yang engine more. That's all fine as long as neither one engine runs over 70% for a lengthy time.

To keep your ship running properly for the long haul, the law of Tai Ji must be followed at all times. That means in a general sense, out of the total Qi produced constantly by both engines, neither engine should run more than 70% while the other falls below 30%. When out of these bounds, the systems of your Life-ship become off-balanced and start to malfunction. If not corrected timely, your ship and the crews are in danger.

For example, a vibrant male captain is more inclined to use more Yang engine for more actions, speed and logical processes. This engine is linked to the ship's internal heating and drying system. You can just imagine. When the ship is over-run by this engine, the pressure is building up, the ship becomes over heated, dried-up, and is subject to detrimental damages to crews' health, systematic explosion and shut down. Results can range from pricy rebuild, permanent losses to total destruction.

On the other hand, a female captain's Life-ship is likely run oppositely. She may prefer more nurturing, healing, creative and artistic processes, which utilize more Yin engine linked to the ship's internal cooling and humidifying system. Can you imagine what happens when this engine is over used? The moisture is building up, the ship becomes colder and colder, and is subject to fungus, rust, damage to crews' health, and systematic malfunctions. Results also can range from pricy repair, permanent damages to total loss.

To avoid these tragedies, simply become mindful and use your less favorite engine more. Perhaps have more resting time or Yin veggies for a Yang warrior Baby Panda and more Yang food or physical activities for a Yin healer Baby Panda. As long as you play with your Yin and Yang engines within this 70/30 boundary, your ship will be powered and operated in a beautiful self-sustaining homeostatic state.

The same rule applies to diet, movements, relationships, businesses, ecosystems and worldly affairs. Going extreme beyond the 70/30 bound in any direction will break this homeostatic state and fall into the abnormal allostatic state, where major disorders, damages and declines begin. Knowing this secret now, my fast learning Baby Panda, you must watch out for extremism in your life, whether it is diet, exercise, attitude, value, religious belief, political view, lifestyle, business venture or financial pursuit. You must watch out for resentful condemnations or dismissals to challenging traits or opposing views of others. Only by equally and truly valuing the attributes and outcomes of both Yin and Yang can you tap into your true potential for deeper connections and greater HAPPY.

Tai Chi = Balancing Yin and Yang within 70/30 Bound = Homeostasis + Harmony = HAPPY

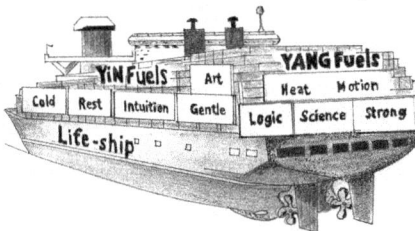

YIN YANG BALANCED LIFE-SHIP

YIN YANG IMBALANCED LIFE-SHIP

🐼 FUN GAME 5: YIN-YANG BALANCE EXAM

Here is the million dollar question, my captain Baby Panda. How are your Life-ship's dual engines running right now?

Momma Panda gives you 3 simple ways to find out:

1. **Resting Heart Rate.** Sit still for at least 5 minutes before checking.

   Group A = 60 – 72/min = within 70/30 bound (Yeah, baby)
   Group B = more than 72/min = too Yang (Your ship is over-heating)
   Group C = less than 60/min = too Yin (Your ship is freezing, unless you are an athlete)

   What's your Resting Heart Rate? _____

2. **Temperature Preference.** Your most comfortable A/C setting at home or in the car during a hot summer

   Group A = 72 – 80° F = within 70/30 boundary (Yeah, baby)
   Group B = less than 72° F = too Yang (Your ship is over-heating)
   Group C = more than 80° F = too Yin (Your Life-ship is freezing)

   What's your favorite temperature? _____

3. **Systolic Blood Pressure.** It is the top number.

   Group A = 80 – 120 = within 70/30 boundary (Yeah, baby)
   Group B = higher than 120 = too Yang (Your ship is burning)
   Group C = less than 80 = too Yin (Your Life-ship is freezing)

   What's your Systolic Blood Pressure? _____

Based on at least 2 out of 3 results, are you in Group A, B or C? _____

If you are in Group A, congrats! If you belong to Group B or C, don't panic. Momma Panda's suggestions on the next page come to your rescue. ☺

FIGURE 3: SUGGESTIONS FOR ENGINE BALANCE

Group A (Yin Yang Balanced): All are fine and dandy with you, my loving and skilled captain Baby Panda. Both engine Yin and engine Yang of your almighty Qi-ship/Life-ship are well fueled and currently running within its 70/30 homeostatic state. Bravo!

Suggestions for the comfy Group A:

1. Continue to give your unconditional love to your families, friends, students, customers, causes, deities and strangers. Yes, continue to stick with your own trueness and peace.

2. Continue to feed your mind and your body with happy and Yin-Yang balanced food. Practice HAPPY TAI CHI™ or any other Meditation or Movement like a born master.

Group B (Too Yang): You love Yang fueling food for your mouth and your mind and you tend to feel hot. Your engine Yang is over running and heating beyond its 70% safety line .If not corrected, your Life-ship will get baked and damaged.

You are not alone, my burning Baby Panda. More than two thirds of the American population has over heated Yang engines. In this overly Yang state, healthy drives can mutate towards aggression and violence, and pleasant desires can grow into greedy obsessions. As introduced in Mindset 2, extreme Yang will inevitably lead to Yin. When your Yang engine is burnt out or compromised, it will cease to operate right and leave your Life-ship falling into coldness and malfunction while waiting for recovery, major repair or replacement. How often have you seen or experienced this crashing phenomenon? A sudden arrival of a cold, flu, fatigue, pain, stroke, heart attack, cancer, ED, depression, bi-polar and other disorders. Too often, my caring Baby Panda, right? Now you understand why I am so compelled to write this book. It's not just for your individual happiness and wellbeing. It's for the survival and wellbeing of our societies, future generations and our whole humanity on Earth.

As severe as it sounds, I am sure you have heard of this saying in English. If there's a will, there's a way. Actually, if you have the will, Momma Panda's ways are pretty simple.

Suggestions for the over-heating Group B:

1. Continue to show your love to your families, friends, students, customers, causes, deities and strangers. While enjoying your own truths and peace, accept and respect others' truths and peace.

2. Cool your Yang engine off and ease on the hot chili pepper, curry spices and anything fried for now.

3. Feed your body more Yin fueling food to turn your Yin engine up. You can use my Yin-Yang Chart for Common Food in my HAPPY TAI CHI™ Diet book or on www.happytaichi.org as a "rough" reference for common food but don't go OCD on it, my Baby Panda. Follow your intuition too.

4. Entertain and experiment with the following suggestions:

   a. Sleep and rest more, at least 8 hours on your day off.
   b. Get 10-min of Moon light each day if possible.
   c. Pray for peace and wellbeing for you, your loved ones and your opponent's.
   d. Listen to jazz, blues, classical or country music whenever you can.
   e. Double up on your favorite Yin engine fueling veggies and clean berries.
   f. Many grains, nuts and fish are cooling food. Eat up. Salmon is Yin-Yang balanced.
   g. Switch your coffee to double green tea for now. If you must sweeten it, a little rock sugar and honey will do.
   h. Take brief relaxation breaks such as sitting meditation, HAPPY TAI CHI™ Pose or Move Meditations during your day, even for just 1 minute at a time.
   i. Let someone get ahead of you in line or on the road.
   j. Let others have the last word.

Group C (Too Yin): You like Yin fueling food for your body and your mind. You tend to feel cold, tired and perhaps melancholy or even sad. Your engine Yin is currently over running beyond 70% bound, my freezing Baby Panda, and your Life-ship is getting too cold and malfunctioning.

Suggestions for the freezing Group C:

1. Continue to show your unconditional love to your families, friends, students, customers, causes, deities and strangers. Find and enjoy your own truth and peace.

2. Slow down your Yin engine and stop any raw diet for now if on any. Reduce Soy product intake for now too.

3. Crank your Yang engine up and feed your body more Yang fueling food. Use my Yin-Yang Chart for Common Food as a rough reference. Never go extreme, my Baby Panda.

4. Entertain and experiment with the following suggestions:

   a. Get 30-min of Sunlight each day if possible, face neck & eyes protected.
   b. Increase your favorite Yang engine fueling meat such as lamb, chicken/turkey and clean shell fish.
   c. For vegetarians, double up on your favorite Yang engine fueling veggies, grains, nuts and seeds.
   d. Spice up your cooking, my creative Baby Panda. Almost all seasonings are warming and heating food.
   e. Eat more stews, baked and slow cooked food.
   f. Spicy and sour flavors are your Yang engine's friends.
   g. Although most sugars and sweeteners are Yang fueling, most fruits are Yin-fueling. So avoid over-eating.
   h. Make sure to be early or on time to your appointments.
   i. Sharpen your focus. Start to make your top 3 lists for the day, week, month and year and focus on them.
   j. Start low-output physical activities such as HAPPY TAI CHI™ Pose Meditations, Level 1 & 2 HAPPY TAI CHI™ Moves, easy Qigong forms, gentle Yoga or walking. Increase progressively when ready.
   k. Listen to disco or dance music whenever you can. Dare to venture some hard rock and metal?
   l. Adopt a hobby, support group, charity cause or a pet that you love. Create some passionate Qi for your ship.

Entertain any suggestions here or pick Yin-Yang fueling food from Momma Panda's 3-layer Cake Food Chart in the HAPPY TAI CHI™ Diet book. Give your engines one month time to cool off or warm up to return to its super homeostatic state. And, my beloved Baby Panda, back to homeostasis they will be.

MINDSET 4: MINIMIZE YOUR QI WASTE

Have you seen a flock of birds flying long distance? They smartly ride the aerodynamic force of air and take turns to lead the pack to conserve their Qi. This is because they are all equipped with the following built-in Tai Chi wisdom:

Better Survival = Qi Conservation = Minimum Waste

Qi conservation is just as important to your survival as to the birds. Each day, your Life-ship requires a certain amount of Qi to keep the crews healthy and departments running. This Qi must be generated from 3 categories as illustrated in Mindset I. Some is from Solar, Lunar, Celestial and Spiritual sources, some is from fellow Life-ships via goodwill or trade, and some is self-produced from air, water and other solid fuels from Earth. Any warfare or major repairs of the ship requires extra Qi.

Ongoing fears and worries of non-life-threatening matters falsely alarm your ship constantly and waste your ship's precious Qi. Having frequent distresses such as resentment, anger, guilt or sadness is like forcing all your crews to carry a dumbbell while they work. Just imagine how exhausting that is to your Qi and your Life-ship.

Remember, my captain Baby Panda, the quality and quantity of your Qi determines the life and death of your crew and ship. To use your Qi efficiently, always be at ease and go with the flow.

In surfing, you go with the flow of the wave. In fighting, you go with the flow of the opponent's force. In running your life-ship, you go with the flow of love.

Love is the least resisted force on Earth. It is like the effortless breeze turning the flowers into fruits, clouds into blue sky and sweats into comfort. Whenever you use its force, you prevail. Whenever you follow its path, you arrive. Whenever you accept its flow, you fulfill.

**Each time you choose to be loving,
you are healing someone;
you are also healing yourself.**

– Momma Panda

We all have had our shares of wounds and injuries on our past ventures, physically and emotionally. Some were small and some were unbearable. Many wounds are still not totally healed and some wounds get frequently re-opened. When people are in great physical pains, they groan in sounds. When people are in great emotional pains, they groan in words. So, please remember, my Baby Panda. At any given moment, everyone is already giving the best as they know how. Take it easy. You have the power to show others and yourself acceptance, love and kindness. This is where resistance, distress and Qi waste stop. This is where healing, growth and HAPPY begin.

Mean words = sounds of pain

Remember, my captain Baby Panda. The signal of love is what links all the Life-ships together. The act of unconditional love is what propels every ship to its final destination – HAPPY.

Minimum Qi Waste = At Ease + Go with the Flow = Go with Love

Life-ship

DON'T GIVE UP YOUR GOODNESS

A man saw a bug floundering around in the water. He decided to save it by stretching out his finger, but the bug stung him. The man still tried to get the bug out of the water, but it stung him again.

On seeing this, his friend told him to stop saving the bug that kept stinging him. The man said: "It is the nature of the bug to sting. It is my nature to love. Why should I give up my loving nature because of the bug's stinging nature?

DONKEY IN THE WELL

One day a farmer's donkey fell down into a well. The animal cried piteously for hours as the farmer tried to figure out what to do. Finally he decided the animal was old and just wasn't worth retrieving, and the well needed to be covered anyway.

So he invited all his neighbors to come over and help him. They all grabbed a shovel and began to shovel dirt into the well. At first, the donkey realized what was happening and cried horribly. Then, to everyone's amazement, he quieted down.

The farmer looked down the well and was astonished at what he saw. With every shovel of dirt that hit his back, the donkey was doing something amazing. He would shake it off and take a step up.

As the farmer's neighbors continued to shovel dirt on top of the animal, he would shake it off and take a step up. Pretty soon, everyone was amazed as the donkey stepped up over the edge of the well and trotted off.

So, remember these stories, my brave Baby Panda. Always keep your loving nature. Should you ever find yourself in a hole and all kinds of dirt are shoveled down on you, just shake it off and keep stepping up. Be at ease and go with the flow of love. It will save your precious Qi for more healing, creativity and HAPPY.

🐼 FUN GAME 6: MINIMIZE YOUR QI WASTE

First, let's go over Momma Panda's tips on conserving your precious Qi.

- Accept all existences, as-is and where-is, whether you understand or approve them at this moment or not.
- Accept your own existence, as-is and where-is, whether you like it or not.
- Simplify your life. Reduce the quantity and improve the quality.
- Do and focus on the things you love that are good for your wellbeing.
- Learn to love overcoming things challenging you. (Yes, you can do it, my Baby Panda! It's for your evolution and HAPPY.)
- Spend time with people you love and who love you.
- Enhance and contribute to the world with what you love.
- Don't be shy, my beloved Baby Panda. Show your love to all - your families, friends, strangers, opponents, animals, plants, oceans, mountains and the whole planet, with no strings attached. Btw, if you are sincere and consistent, you are most likely loved back. ☺
- Align all your life ventures and destinations with love.
- Link all your beliefs with love.
- Operate all your departments and crews with love.

If there is anything really tolling your Qi now, list the top 3 stressors:

1. _____
2. _____
3. _____

Ask yourself these 3 questions:

1) How important is it? _____   2) Is it out of your control? _____

3) Is there an immediate solution? If yes, take action and release the stress.

If not, accept and have peace with it. The sky won't fall. ☺ You can always pray for the outcome you prefer.

MINDSET 5: TUNE UP YOUR NAVIGATIONS

Now that you have learned about your Qi and Life-ship, your dual engines and 70/30 rule and Qi conservation, it's time, my captain Baby Panda, to check and update all the navigation devices and basic operation systems of your ship. To simply put it:

Navigation Systems = Beliefs = Self-Suggestions

It is YOU, the owner and captain, who has the sole power and duty to decide how to run your ship, which programs are most suitable for you, and what locations provide the best eco environment for your ship and crews. If your current navigating system is out-of-date or inaccurate, you now have the choice and power to modify or upgrade at will.

Once upon a time, the ground was thought to be flat and the Sun was thought to go around Earth. Just not long ago, the ancient teaching of "empty state" and "Post-birth Qi can reverse Pre-birth Qi" was considered pure esoteric, and DNA was believed the sole intelligent controller of our biology. Today, quantum physics and epigenetics have proven otherwise. Scientific discoveries have drastically changed the world's belief systems and will continue to do so. We must keep our mind open and systems up-to-date.

It's essential to be mindful from now on that belief determines biology. This means all your beliefs and orders, whether supportive or undermining of your HAPPY, will be faithfully carried out by your crews of your ship.

Belief => Biology
Belief = Placebo/Nocebo => Good/Bad Biology

A patient was told by his doctor that his test result showed that he had 4 months left to live and that he should go home to get his final affairs in order. The patient arranged his affairs and died at the end of 4 months. Later, an autopsy showed that he was given the wrong report. Obviously he believed the doctor and gave his crews the order to shut down the ship in 4 months. The crews carried his order out. This is called Nocebo effect. Any authority in your life can easily download wrong or out-of-date beliefs or apps to your ship's operation system, especially when you were a kid without any "conscious filter".

Another patient was told by his doctor that the operation on his torturing arthritic knee was a success. The scar healed nicely. His pain was all gone and he could play ball again. Actually, nothing was really done on his knee except one cut to show him a scar. But he believed and his crews achieved all the results for him. This is called Placebo effect. Update your beliefs to boost your Qi and best serve your wellbeing. This is an important step to power and guide your ship towards where exactly you desire to go.

Remember, my beloved Baby Panda. All of us are subject to many false, outdated or limiting beliefs and psychological suggestions from the past, which secretly undermine our Yin-Yang balance and Qi usage. Watch out the following frequently seen false beliefs and "navigation defects":

- Self-rejection or self-hatred - one of the internal causes for cancer and other terminal illnesses.
- Perfectionism and "could have done better" syndrome.
- I'm right and my way is the best way and the only way.
- I'm never good enough.
- I must be a certain way or others won't like or approve me.
- I can't be successful (fit, healthy or lovable)
- I must be the center of attention to be happy.
- **I need to earn, buy, date or eat a lot to feel secure and happy.**

In case, you got any of these bugs such as Self-Hatred (or hating others) in your system, without debugging, it will hinder and may override any new self-help app you are trying to install. Knowing is the first step, my Baby Panda. Taking action is the next step. HAPPY TAI CHI™ can help in your daily life through mindset, diet, meditation and/or movement to make sure your navigating systems are efficient, up-to-date, and linked with unconditional love.

Better Navigation = Better Belief = Better Yin-Yang Balancing

🐼 FUN GAME 7: LIST OF YOUR NAVIGATING DEVICES

Your world of reality is built with your beliefs. How you perceive, feel and respond to the outside world is all based on them.

List your current beliefs about you, your life, other people and the world:

I was _____

I am _____

I can be _____

I will be _____

My life was _____

My life is _____

My life can be _____

My life will be _____

My mom is _____

My mom can be _____

My dad is _____

My dad can be _____

My kid is _____

My kid will be _____

My family is _____

My family will be_____

Others are _____

Others will be _____

The world is_____

The world will be_____

🐼 FUN GAME 8: NAVIGATION EXAM & AFFIRMATION

List Beliefs empowering you and bringing HAPPY to you. Re-affirm regularly before eating, during meditation or after waking up. "I am grateful I believe:"

1. _____

2. _____

3. _____

4. _____

5. _____

6. _____

List Beliefs hindering you and making you unhappy. Clarify to yourself these beliefs no longer serve you and it's time to turn the negatives into positives.

1. _____

2. _____

3. _____

Modify these old beliefs such as "I'm a failure" to new ones serving your wellbeing and HAPPY such as "My past failures help me to learn and succeed today." Then re-affirm regularly before eating, during meditation or after waking up. "I am grateful I now believe:"

1. _____

2. _____

3. _____

MINDSET 6: CHOOSE YOUR QI INFLUENCE & UNDERCURRENT

MOM MENG MOVED 3 TIMES

Meng, Ke, was a highly regarded educator, ranked only after "Saint" Confucius in Chinese history. He lost his father at a very young age.

During the mourning period, his mother Mom Meng moved next to the cemetery where Ke's father was buried so she could visit easily. Every day, there were funeral rituals and crying going on. Soon, little Ke began to play his own funeral ritual games with his new friends. They would make small coffins and corpses with mud, carry around and cry. Mom Meng decided to move again.

Meng Ke's new home was right next to a market. To his amusement, from day to night, there were all kinds of people coming and going and all kinds of things happening and visible: men, women, teens, household items, grains, veggies, fruits, fish, meat, butchering, buying, selling, bargaining, cheating, conning, stealing, yelling and fighting. He hung at the market all day. Soon, Little Ke began to copy all he saw. Mom Meng decided to move a third time.

Meng, Ke's new home was next to a school. Every day, students came early and bowed to the teachers; the teachers taught the student songs, poems and respectful manners. Little Ke had been watching and listening each day. Soon, he began to repeat the songs, poems and manners and became interested in learning more and more. Mom Meng did not move again.

One who stays near vermilion gets stained red.
One who stays near ink gets stained black.

– Chinese Parable

As you can see, my beloved Baby Panda, it is very important to examine if the Qi vibrations surrounding your Life-ship and your children's reflect Kindness, Trueness & Peace, and are conducive for learning and growing. If not, make a clear free-will choice inside and take action.

Do you know what happens if you strongly strike a tuning fork on G and then lightly strike another tuning fork on C? If they are close enough, the vibration and sound of C will eventually change to G's vibe and sound. To simply put it:

Stronger Vibration Takes over Weaker Vibration

Each of you, my special Baby Panda, is a custom-made Life-ship, powered with a unique level and symphony of Qi. Since you gather Qi from other Life-ships, when a Life-ship with more Qi amperage and voltage comes by, you are automatically drawn to it. When in close enough range, much like a tuning fork, your tune will begin to converge, knowingly or not, unless you consciously exert greater power to resist. Powerful vibrations in your close living space include:

- Parents, siblings, partners, teachers & besties.
- Leaders, mentors, idols, music & images.
- Drugs, electronic game or smart devices & high voltage power lines.

Are they helpful or harmful? Do their vibrations stand for unconditional love, trueness and peace? If yes, more power to them and join them. If not, their vibes can be discouragement, dishonesty, disrespect, disharmony, depression, sickness, hatred, aggression, violence or even destruction. Unless you are consciously aware and resist all the time, their contradictive vibes will take over yours.

If you'd like, express your choice kindly, honestly and peacefully. If not, disengage and distance yourself or your children from them if possible. If not possible right now, just stand by your choice silently and reaffirm yourself or reassure your children frequently.

In case you are now too weak to resist Life-ship(s) of much stronger Qi vibrating in a toxic frequency close by, how to avoid an undesirable takeover?

Of course you can work on raising your own Qi level ASAP. There are many ways. HAPPY TAI CHI™ can certainly help you on that via its mindset, diet, meditation and/or movement. The easiest and fastest way to become more powerful is to team up with like-minded fellow captains of similar beliefs and Qi vibes. No matter where you are, you will find them. If not locally, you can find support and hobby groups on the internet. Please take the time and effort to find the right one(s), my beloved Baby Panda. It is a Qi investment well worth it for you and your children. Once connected, you can form an invisible collective reservoir of Qi much greater than the Qi of any toxic ones close to you. The more people sharing the same belief in the group, the more magnified this power reservoir can be. Remember, my beloved Baby Panda, 1 little stream may only have so much power. 100 streams merging together and going the same direction become a roaring river. 100 rivers together and going the same direction become an unstoppable tsunami. The same goes with the horsepower of your Qi.

Group Qi Field of Like-Minded People = Qi Undercurrent

The Qi field formed by a big network of collective consciousness with similar vibrations is like a vast hidden undercurrent in the ocean. It can silently turbo charge your Life-ship towards your journey or turn you to a totally different direction. So, even more important than the powerful individuals in your living space, review the job, organization and industry you work for, the group, association and affiliation you belong to, and the neighborhood, society and nation you live in. What are their core vibe and belief? Choose the undercurrent moving your direction. Or, my captain Baby Panda, you will be off your course.

Choose the Qi undercurrents propelling your Life-ship towards your final destination.

🐼 FUN GAME 9: LIST OF POWERFUL QI CLOSE TO YOU

List Loving, Empowering and Nurturing Qi Vibes in your living space:

1. _____   2. _____

3. _____   4. _____

5. _____   6. _____

List Counter-productive or Harmful Qi Vibes in your living space:

1. _____   2. _____

3. _____   4. _____

🐼 FUN GAME 10: LIST OF YOUR QI UNDERCURRENT

Let's screen your group Qi field, my beloved Baby Panda. Keep the ones bringing HAPPY and peace to you. Ditch the ones that hinder your direction. If you can't right away, join and add groups/undercurrents empowering and loving you to strengthen your Qi.

Do they empower you and bring HAPPY to you?   Yes or No

1. Neighborhood & City: _____   _____

2. Workplace: _____   _____

3. Industry/Business Field: _____   _____

4. Group: _____   _____

5. Association: _____   _____

6. Affiliation: _____   _____

7. Other: _____   _____

MINDSET 7: CONFIRM YOUR QUESTS & FINAL DESTINATION

Life is a great adventure game, full of mysterious quests, challenges and rewards. Throughout your journey, so many options of excursions await.

As the new owner and captain, you should review whether the current setting for excursions and destinations reflect YOUR choices and free-will. Here are Momma Panda's recommendations:

- Clear your head before deciding. (HAPPY TAI CHI™ mediation can help. ☺)
- Only set up 1-3 excursions at a time for best focus and productivity.
- Simplify your routes to minimize Qi waste.
- Always afford your crews and ship plenty of time for good quality fuel/food, maintenance, repair and Qi regeneration.
- Only select ventures with rewards you truly love and helpful to your journey. If you take on something to appease another Life-ship, make sure that ship is worth it.
- Always keep your eyes on your ultimate destination.

You already know by now, seeking what you love is your least resisted path. Most of you are already on that path. Whatever you love and seek is all for attaining your HAPPY – the state of happiness. Any unconditional love, kindness, trueness and peace vibrated at you or you vibrated out is a source for your HAPPY. So, my captain Baby Panda, as you are venturing on exciting, relaxing or challenging quests along your life journey, remember where you were from and where you are going. HAPPY is your real home and the ultimate destination.

Final Destination = Your Real Home = HAPPY

🐼 FUN GAME 11: YOUR CURRENT VENTURES

Let's take a look, my Baby Panda. What are your top 3 goals for this year and how do you plan to get there?

Goal 1: _____

How: _____

_____

_____

Goal 2: _____

How: _____

_____

_____

Goal 3: _____

How: _____

_____

_____

Let's venture and have fun, my beloved captain Baby Panda. In the meantime, always remember home.

MINDSET 8: KNOW YOUR "HAPPY"

To me, HAPPY involves feeling any of the following:

Warm & Fuzzy;
Cool & Silly;
Content & Appreciative;
Peaceful & Comfy.
Most of all,
"HAPPY" ⇔ reciprocates with "Smiley"

Whenever I experience a long turbulence in a flight where both my stomach and fear are kicking my butt, I always think of a picture of my son when he was 100 days old. That always turns out to be the most powerful remedy for me, better than any other alternatives such as praying, deep breathing and acupressure. Besides my son, my other favorite sources of HAPPY are:

- Gathering with families, friends and student Baby Pandas
- Sharing Tai Chi and HAPPY with others
- Cooking and/or eating nutritious and delicious food
- Venturing, learning, creating and growing

I am sure you have your own favorite images, moments, people or things that you can think or do to pick you up and keep you sane and going when you are weary, down or in crisis. Your HAPPY always holds more power than any challenges and adversities. It is a magical fuel, catalyst and equalizer for your engines.

You are not a robot, my Baby Panda. Embrace and listen to all your feelings. But, always be sure to remember what brings you to your HAPPY. Because:

What You Feel Now = Your Truth Now = Your Only Reality

One of my favorite movie characters, orphan Maria in the Sound of Music, not only knew what her favorite things were, she also shared with the whole world how she used her treasure chest of "HAPPY" to transform her "Sadness".

36

"Raindrops on roses and whiskers on kittens
Bright copper kettles and warm woolen mittens
Brown paper packages tied up with strings
These are a few of my favorite things

Cream colored ponies and crisp apple strudels
Doorbells and sleigh bells and schnitzel with noodles
Wild geese that fly with the moon on their wings
These are a few of my favorite things

Girls in white dresses with blue satin sashes
Snowflakes that stay on my nose and eyelashes
Silver white winters that melt into springs
These are a few of my favorite things

When the dog bites, when the bee stings
When I'm feeling sad
I simply remember my favorite things
And then I don't feel so bad"

So, know the sources of your HAPPY, my darling beloved Baby Panda, and share its magical effect with your crews and other Life-ships. It's contagious.

Keep in mind. When you consider the ship analogy at a human level, each cell is a crew member; when at a national level, each person is a crew member; when at a planetary level, each nation is a crew member; and when at a galaxy level, each planet is a crew member. HAPPY and Yin-Yang homeostasis work the same way at each level.

Happy Cell =Happy Person = Happy Nation = Happy Planet

"HAPPY" IS AN INSIDE JOB

The Creator gathers all the animals and says:

'I want to hide something most precious from humans until they are ready for it. That is the realization that they create their own reality and HAPPY."

'Give it to me. I'll fly it to the moon," says the Eagle.

'No, soon they will go there and find it."

'How about the bottom of the ocean?'" asks the salmon.

'No, they will find it there too."

'I will bury it in the great plains," says the buffalo.

'They will soon dig and find it there."

'Put it inside them," says the wise grandmother mole.

'Done," says the Creator. *"It is the last place they will look."*

– Native American parable,

So, now you know, my captain Baby Panda. Your life ventures may take you all over the world. But your journey to HAPPY takes place inside of you. ☺

🐼 FUN GAME 12: COUNT YOUR FAVORITE HAPPY

My beloved Baby Panda, breathe slowly and deeply 3 times now. Meditate for a minute or so and begin to go inward and recount. List the things bringing a smile to your face and the "Warm and Fuzzy, Cool and Silly, Content and Appreciative, Peaceful and Comfy" feelings to your heart.

Happy 1: _____

Happy 2: _____

Happy 3: _____

Happy 4: _____

Happy 5: _____

Happy 6: _____

Happy 7: _____

Happy 8: _____

Happy 9: _____

Happy 10: _____

Happy 11: _____

Happy 12: _____

Happy 13: _____

Happy 14: _____

Happy 15: _____

MINDSET 9: SMILE AND BE A HAPPY TAI CHI™ MASTER

WHY "SMILE"?

**Sometimes your joy is the source of your smile,
but sometimes your smile can be the source of
your joy.**

— Thich Nhat Hanh

Like Tai Chi, "Smile" has gotten some serious hidden power of its own for HAPPY. This is why Momma Panda paired up this super "power couple".

Do you know, my beloved Baby Panda, that smiling is actually contagious?[8] The part of your brain that is responsible for your facial expression of smiling when happy or mimicking another's smile resides in the cingulate cortex, an unconscious automatic response area.[9] When you see a smiley face, you have to exert conscious effort not to imitate.[10]

According to researchers, the simple act of smiling produces many benefits to health and happiness. Here are just a few. Smiling can:

- Naturally reduce stress,[11] lift mood, and combat depression[12] without medication. All these will in turn lower heart rate and blood pressure.
- Alleviate pain by releasing your body's natural "pain-killer"[13] without harmful side effects.
- Enhance your look, attractiveness[14] and even longevity.[15]

Next time when a challenge shows up like a blown-up monster, stare right to its face and shoot it with your magical bullets of smile. I guarantee it will deflate like a popped balloon. Or if you'd like, "Hold out the Happy Guitar" (You can learn this HAPPY TAI CHI™ pose in my book, "INDOMITABLE SPIRIT - The HAPPY TAI CHI™ Meditation & Movement".) When at ease and empowered, the right solution will come to you with peace.

My beloved Baby Panda, you are a new-aged old soul. Your journey never ends. In this new venture of HAPPY TAI CHI™, you have:

1. Accepted the Qi reality and taken over your own almighty Life-ship.

2. Gotten to know your Yin & Yang dual engines.

3. Learned how to balance them within 70/30 boundary.

4. Understood how to reduce your Qi waste by being at ease and going with the flow of Love.

5. Fine-tuned all your navigating systems for best result.

6. Grasped how to turbo charge your ship's Qi by choosing the right Qi influence and Qi undercurrent.

7. Reviewed and confirmed your quests & final destination.

8. Most of all, recounted your own favorite sources of HAPPY, which can create your own reality of HAPPY instantly, anywhere and anytime.

You are ready to become that HAPPY TAI CHI™ Master you were born to be – unique, important, indomitable and HAPPY.

As I have discovered and shared with you earlier, my beloved Baby Panda, "HAPPY" is on the top of the wish list for all people around the world. You will find these HAPPY TAI CHI™ mindsets help increase the range of your emotional and physical homeostatic state, put you at ease, and keep you super resilient. More importantly, they add more smiles to your face, your heart and your life.

As you apply your HAPPY TAI CHI™ Mind to your daily living – relationship, diet, business, lifestyle and more, you begin to perceive and experience more and more serenity, harmony and prosperity. Your wellness begins to manifest naturally and your HAPPY begins to emerge easily, at anytime, anywhere and in any situation.

So smile, wherever you are, my beloved HAPPY TAI CHI™ Baby Panda. Whatever earthy quest you are tackling now, join Momma Panda, smile and HAPPY TAI CHI™ it. ☺

HAPPY TAI CHI™ = Tai Chi + Smile

= Greater Homeostasis & Emotional Resilience

= Wellness (Serenity + Harmony + Prosperity)

= Your Ultimate "HAPPY"

FIGURE 4: THE LIST OF TRICKS OF HAPPY TAI CHI™

So far, you have learned HAPPY TAI CHI's secret power to improve your HAPPY as a mindset. In my other books, you will discover that it is a body-mind and wellness-happiness magician with many more "magic tricks" up in its sleeves. Here is a list of ways it can serve your HAPPY:

1. **As a Positive Mindset**, honing homeostasis, efficiency and joy.

2. **As a Relaxation Promoter**, reducing stress and Qi waste, and increasing rejuvenation and longevity.

3. **As an Emotional Resilience Enhancer**, countering anxiety or crisis.

4. **As an Empowering Meditation**, doable lying, sitting or standing, balancing both your Yin and Yang engines.

5. **As a Natural Deep Breathing**, un-forced with HAPPY visuals.

6. **As a Posture Optimizer**, for spine alignment and better mood.

7. **As a Low Impact Physical Exercise**, safely adaptable to your needs.

8. **As an Effective Neuroplasticity Builder**, improving balance, eye-hand coordination, focus and mood.

9. **As a Core Needs Fulfiller**, to your longing for security, rewards and social connections.

10. **As a Harmonious Lifestyle Producer**, balancing your diet, relationship, business and all areas in life.

If you ask a medical professional for the benefits on any one of these items, you will likely get a long list. Here are a short combined summary:

- Decreased stress, anxiety, depression and pain.
- Improved mood, energy, stamina and sleep.
- Improved aerobic capacity, muscle strength and definition.
- Improved flexibility, balance and agility.
- Enhanced bodily systems and normalize blood pressure.
- Improved symptoms of diseases and overall well-being.

Tai Chi practice somehow uniquely umbrellas them all. HAPPY TAI CHI™ just adds a magical smiley face to the powerful equation.

HAPPY TAI CHI™
=
Positive Mindset + Relaxation Promoter + Emotional Resilience Enhancer + Empowering Meditation + Low Impact Physical Exercise + Natural Deep Breathing + Posture Optimizer + Effective Neuroplasticity Builder + Core Needs Fulfiller + Harmonious Lifestyle Producer
+
Smile

When Lao Tsu (Lao Zi 老子), the Taoist forefather, wrote the famous Taoist scripture, Tao Te Ching (Dao De Jing道德经) more than 2600 years ago, I bet he wasn't exactly thinking of any martial art to be created based on the Yin-Yang Tai Chi principles. When the legendary Taoist Master, Zhang San Feng (张三丰), first developed Tai Chi movements about 800 years ago on the dreamy Wudang Mountain, I bet he did not foresee the books of HAPPY TAI CHI™ were coming. If they are in the clouds now watching Momma Panda and all you Baby Pandas benefiting from HAPPY TAI CHI™, I bet they have bigger smiles than all of us.

LAO TSU

ZHANG SAN FENG

HOW TO USE
HAPPY TAI CHI

GREAT TRUTH IS BUT FEW WORDS

The Way gave birth to one;
One gave birth to two;
Two gave birth to three;
Three gave birth to the myriad things.

– Lao Tzu (aka Lao Zi, 6th Century, B.C.)

What does this mean? The answer is coming, my captain Baby Panda. ☺

Your life is an intriguing and mysterious journey. Things can appear totally random and chaotic when you are on the ground amid them. However, as you elevate your view point higher, you begin to see the patterns of orbits you are moving on and those around you. These moving patterns are the same as that of the molecules, atoms and electrons. They are also the same as that of the solar system, milky way and the universe. So, my divine Baby Panda, by now it's easier to recognize the Divine Order you are a part of.

Here are the top 5 divine effectors to your life's journey and quality:

1. **Fate:** Your "secret" predestined orbit & destination.
2. **Luck:** Choices of attractions, detours and speed variations.
3. **Environment/Feng Shui:** Qi/Energy field of home and environment; collective conscious or unconsciousness of group, society and nation.
4. **Karma:** Counter-active force of your calculated or non-calculated deeds.
5. **Education:** Knowledge and wisdoms.

You already know by now that your final destination is your ultimate "HAPPY". Your journey is all about getting there. As you can see, my divine Baby Panda, knowledge will affect your journey for sure. But your choices of attractions, "Qi undercurrents" and actions affect you much more. The fact you choose to read this book now powerfully propels you towards your ultimate "HAPPY".

When a student is ready, the teacher appears.

This book is presenting you one of the simplest ways to approach a seemingly most complicated subject matter – life. My aim is to lay a fundamental understanding for you, my beloved Baby Panda.

Do you know even the most sophisticated computer is coded upon the very two base numbers of "0" and "1"? This is because all things and events in our world, including your Life-ship, are outcomes of the balancing play of Qi's two powering engines, Yin and Yang, no matter how complicated they appear on the surface. Or, in modern terms, all occurrences are just the fluxing manifestations between the "homeostatic" and "allostatic" states of the myriad things, from cells, diets, health, physical activities, social connections, world affairs, ecosystems to galaxies. No exceptions.

Heaven needs Yin and Yang;
Earth needs softness and hardness;
Humanity needs mercy and justice;
These Three Marvels are interrelated and
based on the balance of the two opposites.

– I Ching (Book of Change, 24th Century B.C.)

The ancient Yin-Yang Tai Chi understanding is but one of human's early revelations and insights into the basic truths about the operations of our world, from the atom to the universe. Science is definitely catching on.

So, here is the answer, my beloved Baby Panda:

The Way = the Divine Order;
One = Qi, the Energy;
Two = Yin and Yang, the Dual Engines;
Three = Heaven, Earth and Humanity, the Three Marvels.

The Divine gave birth to Qi:
Qi gave birth to Yin and Yang;
Yin and Yang gave birth to Heaven, Earth and Humanity;
Heaven, Earth and Humanity gave birth to the myriad things.

FIGURE 5: WORLDLY HEALTH & HEALING SYSTEMS

Throughout the history of mankind, branches of more detailed knowledge and wisdoms for health and happiness have been pursued and discovered by numerous timeless spirits, ingenious minds and capable bodies all over the world. Here's Momma Panda's short list of the most practiced today:

1. Western Medicine & Psychology System

2. Oriental Medicine & 5-Element System

3. Ayurveda Medicine & 3-Humor System

4. Homeopathic Medicine System

5. Naturopathy Medicine System

6. Holistic & Alternative Healing Systems:

    - Quantum, Biofeedback and Vibrational Medicine.
    - Native American Medicine & Amazon/Shaman Medicine.
    - Qigong, Reiki & all other Energy Healing Systems.
    - Healing Touch, Massage Therapy & Reflexology.
    - Sound, Color, Aroma, Hydro, Laugh & Colonic Therapy.
    - **Psychic & Dream Healing and more.**

Once a fundamental running program for all things is understood, you can easily use any of these more detailed health and healing apps for your unique Life-ship's operational need. Just choose any one or a few you feel most drawn to. No matter which helper(s) you choose and whether you are approaching from body, mind or spirit, or any 2 or 3 of them all at once, the aim is to efficiently restore and strengthen your homeostasis or Yin-Yang balance (Tai Chi). When the Yin-Yang balance is regained and maintained, the ultimate goal to bring you home to HAPPY can be more easily attained.

FIGURE 6: WHO CAN "HAPPY TAI CHI™"?

This book provides you essential awareness and mindset to attain your HAPPY. My other HAPPY TAI CHI™ books offer insight and tips on diet, meditation and movement to enhance your wellness and HAPPY. Whatever your age, gender, role and task are, you will find HAPPY TAI CHI™ easily usable for you or loved ones to improve HAPPY on each of your unique journeys.

YOU

My precious Baby Panda, whether you are mentioned in this section or not, you are YOU, like no one else on Earth. You were equipped with your kindness, genuineness and will to grow at birth, and powered by love and compassion after you were born. You are summoned here on a mission that only you can figure out. Forest Gump's mother told him at her death bed that she was destined to be his momma and she did the best she could. You too have been giving your best each day and every time to learn and grow. HAPPY TAI CHI™ is just a very special precious gem you discovered along the way to be your tool, fuel, cheerleader, secret trainer and sorcerer, whichever you are in need of each time.

The Warrior in all of us

We all have a warrior inside, whether a hidden dragon or a crouching tiger, dormant at the moment or out battling already. HAPPY TAI CHI™ mindsets, poses and movements connect you to your inner fighter, strengthen its power, harmonize its urges and harness its flow. This book will transform you into the Master of your courageous warrior within, as you were always intended and destined to be.

Lay People or Non-Asian Folks

If you never heard of the word Tai Ji or Tai Chi, have limited knowledge in Asian culture or philosophy and are not a martial art or fitness enthusiast, this book is written with you in mind. It will add a few new words, useful concepts and invaluable insights to your worldly vocabularies and narratives. By simply incorporating a few things from the HAPPY TAI CHI™ Mindset and Diet to your life or just 8 reps of Happy Cloud Hands or any other movements during TV commercials each day, this book will change your life FOREVER, for the better.

Pro Athletes, Dancers, Martial Artist or MMA Fighters

If you are a pro, this book will sharpen your edge by enabling you to be more superiorly resilient both in body and mind. Each HAPPY TAI CHI™ movement provides fluid multi-plane isometric and stretching training, deep breathing and meditative benefits in a highly energy-conserving way. Adding some HAPPY TAI CHI™ mindsets, diet and movements to your cross training regimens will balance and hone your neural pathways for greater performance and thresholds.

Business Professionals & Office Workers

If you work in an office or cubicle without fresh air, chances are there are very few negative ions in your space to carry fresh energy to you. You may feel low energy more easily compared to working outside. You will find doing one or a few of your favorite HAPPY TAI CHI™ poses or movements in sitting or standing position can boost your mood and energy level like a charm. You can even stay on the speaker phone while you move or hold a cool HAPPY TAI CHI™ pose like a pro. Give it a shot.

Artists, Designers, Writers & Music Composers

When you are in the creative space, a free flow of new ideas and inspirations are essential as to the ability to manifest and execute. HAPPY TAI CHI™ facilitates both. If you feel stagnant, do some HAPPY TAI CHI™ moves to get flow going again. If you feel overwhelmed, HAPPY TAI CHI™ pose meditation will help harmonize your creative Qi and choreograph them into another masterpiece.

Moms-to-Be

If you are building a YOU 2.0 inside of you right now, every string of vibration of energy supplied from you is woven in. Your beliefs, temperament, lifestyle and food habits are all being taken in as building blocks. Remember, my Baby Panda, "perceptions determine biology" and "the apple does not fall too far from the tree." Though the initial look and structure are 50/50 up to you, your baby's initial temperaments and habits are almost entirely in your hands. HAPPY TAI CHI™ practice will help keep your spirit joyful, mind resilient and body balanced during this special time to ensure optimal input from you to your next generation.

The New Parents

If you are a brand new parent, unless somebody else is doing all the work, you are probably feeling tired or exhausted right now from your duties, caution and lack of sleep, especially a nursing mom. Between hormonal change after birth and continued adrenaline release due to over protection, the body's energy level is already taking a huge dive. Sleep deprivation can easily lower it down to a depression level. Just practicing 1 minute of any HAPPY TAI CHI™ pose or movement will bring you right to your HAPPY place and switch your bodily system from stress (red light) state to relaxation (green light) state for recovery. It will hone your ability to remain calm and resilient and conserve your very valuable energy while dealing with your baby "adventure".

Adolescents & Kids

After the age of 12, you start to have more and more of your own beliefs and thoughts about things. Some may be different from your care givers' or the authorities'. Inability to make decisions for yourself and having to follow orders can make you feel powerless and frustrated inside. Growing hormone fluxes during these teenage years definitely makes it even more challenging. Of course you can channel these feelings through "emo" and "screamo" music and attires. This book will help you capture this growing power inside of you and alchemize it into your great vision and resolve for your creativity and future endeavors.

For younger kids, a quick 1-3 minutes HAPPY TAI CHI™ break during any class or homework time affords a productive exercise and relaxation recess. It will boost their neural activities, concentration skills and emotional resilience.

Seniors

Whether you are living by yourself, with your kids, or at a facility, the goals for most of you may be less medications, better quality of life and longevity. Nicknamed as "Medication in Motion", HAPPY TAI CHI™ pose or movement is safe and effective for almost all conditions and can be practiced lying, sitting, standing or moving, very briefly or extensively based on your situation. When combined with its Mindset and Dietary Guide, HAPPY TAI CHI™ can easily be one of your best companions to all your current programs, procedures, treatments or medications.

Military, Law Enforcement & Veterans

As a proud Army/Green Beret mom, I solute you all and feel extra close to you. I can only imagine the pressure you endure under extreme training and real life-threatening circumstances. Some of you suffered temporary or permanent bodily injuries and damages. Regular HAPPY TAI CHI™ practice is proven to ease chronic pain, reduce mood disturbances, decrease anxiety, combat depression, and instill inner peace. Some of you have a hard time switching off your mental "fight-or-flight" button after the dangers are long over. The unwanted release of adrenaline and cortisol causes disruption to the healthy balance and function of your body and mind. HAPPY TAI CHI™ practices release positive neural transmitters and bio-chemicals such as endorphin, serotonin and dopamine, reconnecting and strengthening the neural pathways associated with your HAPPY sources. It will help improve and restore your emotional balance and resilience.

Chronic Worriers

If you worry the sky may fall and Earth may explode, I'd say that won't happen in your life time. If you worry you will be sick, your son will be mate-less, and bad things will always happen to you, these "wishes" may just come true soon. Consistent worry is like "cursing" bad outcomes at yourself and others. Your fearful and nervous energy also programs and influences your kids and spouse. HAPPY TAI CHI™ mindsets, diets, along with its simple poses or moving meditations, can all help bring about and re-enforce your serenity and liberate you from the bondage of fear and worries.

The Sick and Disabled

You must be a super strong person if you have endured crippling viruses, corrupted genes or other disabilities since birth or due to sickness or accident. When I met the Parkinson's and post-polio groups of Boca Raton, I was so inspired by them. For every little thing we can easily do and think nothing of, they have to put out such extra efforts. But they do it as if it's also nothing for them. HAPPY TAI CHI™ can definitely help ease chronic pain, keep your body more coordinated, toned, agile as long as possible, and add smiles and quality to your life.

For those who have temporary diseases such as flus and colds, malfunctioning organs and bodily systems, you must know that these are NOT permanent. Whatever beliefs, temperaments, habits, diets and lifestyles that got you there can be modified and reversed over time so these outcomes and symptoms can be improved or eliminated. HAPPY TAI CHI™ can be a safe and simple helper and power-tool for your recovery.

Sometimes, you choose to be sick because you long for attention and love. Or you just need some relief from ongoing overwhelming demands and responsibilities. This choice may stem from your conscious or sub-conscious. A sick day now and then is no biggie. But doing this on a regular basis may not serve your best interest, my beloved Baby Panda. Various sick rehearsals and medications may eventually take a permanent toll on your body and mind. Please consider these alternatives for relief: Express yourself, get a pet or a stuffed animal, underwhelm your life, and practice HAPPY TAI CHI™.

The Anxious

When you are eaten up by anxiety, someone or something at present or in the past must be troubling the hell of you, beyond what you currently can handle. You feel powerless, hopeless and probably breathless too. It's a traumatic experience. Persisted occurrences often lead to unwanted somatic disorders, emotional issues, and uncontrollable compulsions or body movements. This someone or something may not improve at this time. But HAPPY TAI CHI™ can instantly connect you to your sources to HAPPY and improve your bio-chemicals and neural pathways. It will enable you to handle more challenges and remain calm. As you get stronger and more peaceful within, this someone or something won't seem that terrifying any more. Anxiety attacks will lessen and be eliminated over time. So will the unwanted stuff caused by it.

The Depressed

When unwanted situations appear not going away anytime soon and you can't see a way out, you may feel consumed and hopelessly trapped by it. You may feel the darkness has befallen. Remember, my beloved Baby Panda. The sun can be temporarily behind the cloud, but it's always there. Fear not and despair not. Your sun will come out and shine again. Do not let the challenges take your power and confidence away. Do not let your dislike of the situation and fear of the future waste your energy away. It's time to persevere and improvise. Ask for help, join a support group and shut down self-criticism. HAPPY TAI CHI™ is here to rid your blues by reconnecting you with your sunny energy inside.

The Addicted

If you fear to face undesirable situations or want to escape from the intolerable feeling of anxiety, there are many options. Getting wasted with booze and drugs or burying your head in the sand of work, sex, shopping or food are some of the most well-known. Whichever you selected did the trick and eased your anxiety momentarily. With the help of surrounding enablers, advocates and victims, you were able to do it again and again until your mind formed a new neural pathway, your body formed a new biochemical balance and you formed a new addictive "habit". HAPPY TAI CHI™ tackles your habit from the root by easing your painful anxiety and switching your link directly to your body's natural HAPPY and "high". It trains your mind and body to create new pathways and balances for a more resilient and capable you.

The Perfectionist and Overly Critical

As you know now, the healthy and happy range for errors or omissions is within the 70/30 bound, just like everything else. Either too high or too low begins to make us less human. Please remember. At any given time, everyone is already giving the best Qi output from each one's uniquely combined capacity of subconscious and conscious, whether others comprehend or not. "You could have done better" is a sabotaging belief and a bar neither you nor anyone else can reach. If while growing up, you were given this belief and standard, it can be exhausting forcing yourself and others to chase that mirage. Here are some navigation updates: accept and validate the current whereabouts of yourself and others, put the bar at "you can do better next time", and practice HAPPY TAI CHI™ to increase unconditional love and HAPPY.

The Socially Awkward

Everyone is given different talents and challenges in the game of life. In today's diverse world, all of us may feel unsure of what to say or do to others from time to time. HAPPY TAI CHI™ doesn't provide practical scripts for all your social scenarios. It does provide effective ways to increase your ease and resilience level. If you are taking a HAPPY TAI CHI™ pose or movement break, others may be intrigued into a conversation or join you. So, it builds happiness for yourself and bonding connections with other like-minded people. Hey, my talented single Baby Panda, let's test HAPPY TAI CHI™ as your new pickup line next time, and let me know what happens.

The Bullies

If you feel the urge to vent your frustrations and pain insde on someone weaker than you, you must have been bullied now or before by someone stronger than you. You were vulnerable and helpless just like the one you are bullying now. You can't change the past and may not have the power to control your current bully. But, my brave Baby Panda, you have the power to stop this pattern on its track, now. HAPPY TAI CHI™ helps heal your pain and channel your pent up energy into forces for great creativity and compassion. Sing, dance, run, jump, write, paint and design your heart out. Become a big bro or sis to share your courage with other weak and vulnerable.

The Victims

When you are forced to accept unfair treatment or embarrassment by mental or physical coercion or abuse, the feeling of humiliation and injustice can eat you alive. When no instant solution seems available, the powerless feeling is even more crippling. Don't wither, my beloved Baby Panda. Many things can damage your flesh but nothing and no one can destroy your spirit and soul. Whether you believe in Karma, science or a higher power, pray for the abuser's recovery and pray for you to forgive. Remember, all abusers most likely are also victims of prior abuses. HAPPY TAI CHI™ empowers you from inside out and brings healing and peace to you.

Intellectual, Spiritual, Metaphysical & New Age Devotees

If you have a keen devotion to intellect and spirituality, you may spend a lot of your time sitting down, reading, writing, praying, meditating, chanting and doing healing works for others. While peace and bliss feel out of this world, my devoted Baby Panda, don't forget about your earthly body. It's said Dharma created martial art moves to revitalize the withering limbs of the devoted monks who sat and meditated all day. Let HAPPY TAI CHI™'s simple and effective movements and poses balance your whole system and keep your body as vibrant as your spirit and mind.

The Religious and Believers of Celestial Deities

If you follow an organized religion or believe in a celestial deity, you are not alone. Many people on Earth share your beliefs. They usually follow certain moral guidance, practice rituals and pray regularly. Some aim to return to their holy celestial homeland when their earthy missions are over. Whichever group you belong, please remember, my spiritual Baby Panda. Religions are meant to enlighten and guide people towards human's True Natures, i.e., Acceptance (Equality), Kindness (Goodwill), Trueness (Genuineness), Compassion (Unconditional Care) and Peace (Harmonious Existence).

When Yin and Yang engines are balanced and things are in its homeostatic state, these natures are easily manifested and extended everywhere. When Yin and Yang engines are over heated and things are getting extremely polarized and falling out of the homeostatic state, we will see rejection, cruelty, phoniness, greed and war everywhere. Any cults of extremism are like cancer cells. They cannot even grow when Yin and Yang engines are balanced and things are in its homeostatic state. This is just how Qi works in our world.

We may look, sound and appear to be very different on the surface. But when we look deeper at a cellular level, our differences become so minimal, no matter what we believe or not believe. HAPPY TAI CHI™ practice helps enhance your own Yin-Yang balance and spiritual journey. More importantly, it nurtures your understanding and compassion towards other religions, believers and nonbelievers, and promotes more peace and HAPPY for all.

TAKE ACTION NOW

No two drifting snowflakes look the same.
But they all melt on your nose the same.
Here and now.

– Momma Panda

Past is a history. Future is a mystery. Let go any depression over the past and any anxiety over the future. Be present, my captain Baby Panda. "Here and now" is only what you truly possess.

Reload your HAPPY now!

Ten great ideas are not as good as one action. Make the best out of Momma Panda's HAPPY TAI CHI™. Take action and recode your mind for more "HAPPY". Better yet, discover and apply your own special HAPPY prescriptions. I can't wait to hear your HAPPY TAI CHI stories!

MOMMA PANDA WILL ALWAYS BE HERE, CHEERING YOU ON! ☺

BOOKS & TRAINING EVENTS BY MASTER YU

The following publications and courses are available at www.happytaichi.org for viewing, pre-registration or ordering.

A portion of all proceeds will be donated to Yu School, a nonprofit entity formed by Master Yu to provide Tai Chi, Qigong and wellness education to the public, especially those underserved and less fortunate.

Publications

THE SECRET POWER OF HAPPY TAI CHI™
– A New Playbook for Today's Happy & Healthy Living
[Movements Optional]
(Limited edition Book & E-Book, available only at classes and seminars, released Dec. 2017)

"HAPPY" – Reloaded
Recode Your Mind for Modern Happy Living
[THE HAPPY TAI CHI™ MIND]
(Book & E-Book, released on Amazon in Feb. 2018)

FREEDOM – Reclaimed
[THE HAPPY TAI CHI™ DIET & PRESCRIPTION]
(Book & E-Book to be released on Amazon in early 2018)

INDOMITABLE SPIRIT
[THE HAPPY TAI CHI™ MEDITATION & MOVEMENT]
(Book, E-Book, CD & DVD to be released on Amazon in early 2018)

HAPPY TAI CHI™ BENEFITS
(FREE E-Book, available at www.happytaichi.org)

Training

HAPPY TAI CHI™ SEMINAR
(3 Hours, national tour starting in spring of 2018)

HAPPY TAI CHI™ INSTRUCTOR TRAINING & CERTIFICATION
(9 Hours, national tour starting in spring of 2018)

HAPPY TAI CHI™ CEU COURSE
(6 Hours, available in later 2018)

To invite Master Jennifer Yu (Momma Panda) to your organization or event for lecture, seminar or instructor training on HAPPY TAI CHI™, please contact **event@ happytaichi.org.**

To attend one of Master Jennifer Yu's HAPPY TAI CHI seminars, courses and/ or instructor training, go to **www.happytaichi.org/event** to register online, or contact **info@happytaichi.org** for more info.

To contribute to Yu School's "Wellness-for-ALL" mission, please feel free to donate any money, space, time and skills. You can also do your Amazon shopping through Yu School's link on **www.yuschool.com/donate.** Yu School will get a few percent back on your order from Amazon.

For more information on HAPPY TAI CHI™ and Yu School, please check out **www. happytaichi.org** and **www.yuschool.com.**

Thank you for becoming my beloved Baby Panda.

Thank you for being a part of **Master Yu/Momma Panda's mission.**

REFERENCES

1. Shimoff, Marci and Kline, Carol (2008). "Happy for No Reason, 7 Steps to Being Happy from the Inside Out." (pp. 12)"

2. Willett, W. C. (2002). "Balancing Life-Style and Genomics Research for Disease Prevention." *Science* 296: 695-698.

3. Kopp, M. S. and J. Rethelyi (2004). "Where psychology meets physiology: chronic stress and premature mortality-the Central-Eastern European health paradox." *Brain Research Bulletin* 62: 351-367.

4. McEwen, B. S. and T. Seeman (1999). "Protective and Damaging Effects of Mediators of Stress: Elaborating and Testing the Concepts of Allostasis and Allostatic Load." *Annals of the New York Academy of Sciences* 896: 30-47.

5. McEwen, B. and with Elizabeth N. Lasley (2002). "The End of Stress As We Know It". Washington, National Academies Press.

6. Segerstrom, S. C. and G. E. Miller (2004). "Psychological Stress and the Human Immune System: A Meta-Analytic Study of 30 Years of Inquiry." *Psychological Bulletin* 130(4): 601-630.

7. "We hold these truths to be self-evident, that all Men are created equal, that they are endowed by their Creator with certain unalienable rights that among these are Life, Liberty, and the Pursuit of Happiness." The second paragraph in the *Declaration of Independence of the United States.*

8. Primitive emotional contagion. Hatfield, Elaine; Cacioppo, John T.; Rapson, Richard L. Clark, Margaret S. (Ed), (1992). "Emotion and social behavior". *Review of personality and social psychology*, Vol. 14. (pp. 151-177). Thousand Oaks, CA, US: Sage Publications, Inc, xi, 311 pp.

9. O'Doherty, J., Winston, J., Critchley, H. Perrett, D., Burt, D.M., and Dolan R.J., (2003) "Beauty in a smile: the role of medial orbitofrontal cortex in facial attractiveness". *Neuropsychologia*, 41, 147–155.

10. Sonnby–Borgström, M. (2002), "Automatic mimicry reactions as related to differences in emotional empathy". *Scandinavian Journal of Psychology*, 43: 433–443.

11. Seaward BL. "Managing Stress: Principles and Strategies for Health and Well-Being". Sudbury, Mass.: *Jones and Bartlett*; 2009:258.

12. Karren KJ, et al. "Mind/Body Health: The Effect of Attitudes, Emotions and Relationships". New York, N.Y.: *Benjamin Cummings*, 2010:461.

13. R.D. (2000). "Neural correlates of conscious emotional experience". In R.D. Lane & L. Nadel (Eds.), *Cognitive neuroscience of emotion* (pp. 345–370). New York: Oxford University Press.

14. "Facial attractiveness: evolutionary based research" *Phil Trans R Soc B* June 12, 2011 366: 1638-1659.

15. Abel E. and Kruger M. (2010) "Smile Intensity in Photographs Predicts Longevity," *Psychological Science*, 21, 542–544.

DETAILED CONTENTS

ACKNOWLEDGEMENTS

1. My gratitude goes to all my masters and teachers who introduced and taught me the movements, techniques and knowledge of Tai Chi, which have secretly kept me resilient and positive in the face of death and all my adversities in life, and to all my students who have kept me going and inspired along the way.

2. My thanks go to all the unsung heroes who donated their precious time to take photographs, draw illustrations, and provide editing and proofing over and over again for this book, and to all the unsung heroes of Tai Chi and Happiness researchers. All their hard work has made this book possible.

3. I thank the divine for the gift of my families, especially my son, who have enabled me to understand, feel and give unconditional love – my infinite fountain of HAPPY, and for all the challenges in my life which propelled my personal growth and my journey toward altruism, kindness, trueness and inner peace – the ultimate sources for HAPPY.

ABOUT MASTER YU
THE "MOMMA PANDA"

Master Jennifer Wenhong Yu is an international wellness activist, mentor and a 6th generation Tai Chi Master of China's Yang Family Tai Chi Chuan Lineage. She holds a Master's degree in Healtheology in the U.S. and an Economic Law degree from Peking University, China. She is well versed in eastern wellness as well as western fitness and was a former examiner, personal trainer and advanced instructor of Therapeutic Yoga and Pilates.

Master Yu started her Tai Chi journey 30 years ago at Peking University's championship martial art team. Immigrated to the U.S. in 1989, she has personally taught tens of thousands of students.

As an abuse survivor and a former Al-Anon member, Ms. Yu founded Yu School, a non-profit entity to bring Tai Chi's renowned healing and health benefits to everyone, especially those who are suffering and underserved.

Master Jennifer W. Yu loves her family and students, and is a proud Green Beret mom. Besides planning and conducting her national tours of HAPPY TAI CHI™ seminars, CEU courses and instructor certification, she enjoys training instructors and teaching classes to both public and private students in Boca Raton, Florida, where she currently lives, just minutes from her loving family.

Momma Panda/ Master Jennifer W. Yu

www.ingramcontent.com/pod-product-compliance
Lightning Source LLC
Chambersburg PA
CBHW072210090426
42740CB00012B/2459